HER EXISTENCE
IGNORANCE OF WOUND

SUMEET KUMAR

Copyright © Sumeet Kumar
All Rights Reserved.

This book has been self-published with all reasonable efforts taken to make the material error-free by the author. No part of this book shall be used, reproduced in any manner whatsoever without written permission from the author, except in the case of brief quotations embodied in critical articles and reviews.

The Author of this book is solely responsible and liable for its content including but not limited to the views, representations, descriptions, statements, information, opinions and references ["Content"]. The Content of this book shall not constitute or be construed or deemed to reflect the opinion or expression of the Publisher or Editor. Neither the Publisher nor Editor endorse or approve the Content of this book or guarantee the reliability, accuracy or completeness of the Content published herein and do not make any representations or warranties of any kind, express or implied, including but not limited to the implied warranties of merchantability, fitness for a particular purpose. The Publisher and Editor shall not be liable whatsoever for any errors, omissions, whether such errors or omissions result from negligence, accident, or any other cause or claims for loss or damages of any kind, including without limitation, indirect or consequential loss or damage arising out of use, inability to use, or about the reliability, accuracy or sufficiency of the information contained in this book.

Made with ♥ on the Notion Press Platform
www.notionpress.com

Sumeet Kumar

Sumeet Kumar is a writer whose life beautifully reflects the journey of love, struggle, and self-belief. Throughout his life, he has stumbled many times, yet every fall only made him rise stronger. His experiences, rich in emotion and resilience, flow naturally into his writing — making each word feel deeply personal and real.

Alongside writing, Sumeet also finds his rhythm in music. A passionate singer by hobby, his voice carries the same sincerity and emotion that his words convey. Whether through melodies or stories, his creations echo the truths of life and the beauty of human feeling.

Known as a "writer of the new era," Sumeet began his literary journey at a remarkably young age — while still in school. His works blend modern thought with heartfelt expression, capturing the pulse of today's generation and leaving a lasting impression on readers.

In his writing, one finds the tenderness of love, the reality of life, and the power of inspiration woven together with grace. Sumeet Kumar is not just a writer — he is a voice that resonates with every heart that has ever loved, lost, and found itself again.

Contents

Foreword	*ix*
Preface	*xi*
Acknowledgements	*xiii*
Prologue	*xv*
1. THE SILENCE	1
2. THE INVISIBLE EXISTENCE	2
3. THE SUPPRESSED VOICE	3
4. THE BROKEN FAITH	4
5. THE SOCIAL PRISON	5
6. THE WOUNDS YOU DON'T SEE	6
7. THE CAGED DREAMS	7
8. THE GOD WHO FAILED	8
9. THE WOMAN AS THE WORLD	9
10. HER VOICE WILL NOT DIE	10
11. THE UNSEEN HUMAN	11
12. THE SILENCE OF HER VOICE	12
13. THE BODY THAT CARRIES THE WORLD	13
14. THE DOMESTIC PRISON	14
15. THE SOCIETY OF DOUBLE FACES	15
16. THE MOTHER WHO RAISED THE WORLD	16
17. THE SHAME SHE NEVER ASKED FOR	17
18. HE EDUCATION SHE WAS DENIED	18
19. THE SOCIAL MEDIA CIRCUS	19
20. THE WOMAN AS THE WARRIOR	20
21. THE WOMAN AND THE GOD	21
22. THE REBIRTH OF HER VOICE	22

Contents

23. THE WOMAN IS THE WORLD	23
24. SUFFER LONG	24
25. THE BENEATH	25
26. THE VOICE BENEATH THE SILENCE	26
27. THE CHAINS OF EXPECTATION	27
28. THE SCARS THEY NEVER SEE	28
29. THE UNHEARD CRIES	29
30. THE BODY THAT CARRIES SHAME	30
31. THE DREAMS IN CHAINS	31
32. THE BROKEN SOCIETY	32
33. THE WOMAN WHO STILL BELIEVES	33
34. THE FIRE INSIDE	34
35. THE MIRROR OF HUMANITY	35
36. THE WOMAN WHO RISES	36
37. THE WOMAN AND THE SKY	37
38. THE UNHEARD HEARTBEAT	38
39. THE BIRTH OF EXPECTATION	39
40. THE WEIGHT OF DUTY	40
41. THE INVISIBLE SCARS	41
42. THE STOLEN DREAMS	42
43. THE BODY AND THE BURDEN	43
44. THE CHAOS OF SOCIETY	44
45. THE WOMAN WHO STILL LOVES	45
46. THE BROKEN VOICES	46
47. THE RAGE OF RESURRECTION	47
48. THE FIRE OF CHANGE	48

Contents

49. THE MEN WHO LEARNED	49
50. THE WOMAN AND THE SKY	50
51. BORN TO SHINE	51
52. HER SILENCE	52
53. HIDES A STORM	53
54. CARRY STORIES	54
55. WRAPPED IN SKIN	55
56. SHE REWROTE	56
57. SILENCE GROW	57
58. STRENGTH IS A LIE	58
59. CHAINED HER FEET	59
60. UNSPOKEN PRAYERS	60
61. REBIRTH	61
62. I AM THE HOME	62
63. POURS KINDNESS	63
64. AGAINST SILENCE	64
65. READ BY THE BLIND	65
66. BECOMES THE ARROW	66
67. EQUAL TO THE SKY	67
68. HER EMOTIONAL	68
69. HEARTBEAT OF HUMANITY	69
70. SOUND OF SURVIVAL	70
71. MEANING OF FREEDOM	71
72. HER PAST	72
73. HEAVEN BOWS	73
74. BEGINING OF LOVE	74

Contents

EPILOGUE – THE ETERNAL WOMAN   75

Foreword

First of all, I wholeheartedly thank all of you for choosing me.
I do not know why you chose me, but I do know this much — my readers are not just readers; they are a part of my existence.
I am just an artist, but my real art is all of you, who have deemed me worthy of presenting my emotions, my words, and my thoughts before you.
My only request to you is to embrace this book with the same love, the same connection, and the same intimacy as you have embraced my previous works.

— Sumit Kumar

Preface

They say every story begins with a dream — but what if the dream is buried before it even breathes?
I have seen women live without living, speak without being heard, and smile while bleeding within.
This is not a story of one woman; it is the voice of millions whose throats have been tied with the rope of society's expectations.
   This is not fiction. This is truth dressed as a narrative.
This is her — the woman who raised the world, and still, the world questions her existence.
   Every society writes rules, but few write justice.
Every home has walls, but few have hearts.
And every woman carries a story — a story no one asks about.
   I have seen the pain of being a woman, the courage it takes to wake up every morning, and the silent wars she fights every night.
This story is not a tale — it's a confession of generations.
It's not an attempt to prove anything; it's a reflection of what already exists — hidden in plain sight.
   This book belongs to her — the woman who stands quietly behind every success, who is both the wound and the healer.
She is not just part of this world; she is this world.

Acknowledgements

Sumeet Kumar

Sumeet Kumar is a writer whose life beautifully reflects the journey of love, struggle, and self-belief. Throughout his life, he has stumbled many times, yet every fall only made him rise stronger. His experiences, rich in emotion and resilience, flow naturally into his writing — making each word feel deeply personal and real.

Alongside writing, Sumeet also finds his rhythm in music. A passionate singer by hobby, his voice carries the same sincerity and emotion that his words convey. Whether through melodies or stories, his creations echo the truths of life and the beauty of human feeling.

Known as a "writer of the new era," Sumeet began his literary journey at a remarkably young age — while still in school. His works blend modern thought with heartfelt expression, capturing the pulse of *today's generation and leaving a lasting impression on readers.*

In his writing, one finds the tenderness of love, the reality of life, and the power of inspiration woven together with grace. Sumeet Kumar is not just a writer — he is a voice that resonates with every heart that has ever loved, lost, and found itself again.

Prologue

In a world where noise is louder than feelings, her silence screamed the most.

She sat by the window, looking at the same street where she had walked barefoot as a child — with dreams as high as the clouds.

Now, those same feet wore anklets of rules, tradition, and judgment.

She wasn't born weak; she was made to believe she was.

Every voice she tried to raise was crushed under the weight of "What will people say?."

Every dream she dared to see was buried under the eyes of those who called themselves protectors.

That night, she whispered to herself —

"I am not just a woman. I am the foundation on which your pride stands."

ONE
THE SILENCE

The night was quiet, yet her heart screamed louder than thunder.
She sat near the half-lit window, the moon's shadow kissing her bruised hand.
Outside, the street dogs barked — as if warning the darkness that someone still dared to survive it.
   Inside, she whispered to herself:
   "I am the voice that you tried to silence.
I am the wound that refuses to bleed anymore.
I am every woman you forgot to remember."
   She wasn't asking for freedom anymore; she was becoming it.

TWO
THE INVISIBLE EXISTENCE

People nowadays do not consider a woman a human being.
They think she is an object, a worker, a caretaker, a listener, a servant of emotions.
She can cook, clean, raise children, tolerate anger, accept insult — but if she dreams, she is wrong.
If she speaks, she is loud.
If she stays quiet, she is weak.
    Who made this society?
Was it one man?
Or was it all of us, silent participants of this cruelty?
    Every woman's breath is taxed by judgment.
She is told —
    "You are a girl. Behave like one."
    But no one tells her what it truly means to be human.

THREE
THE SUPPRESSED VOICE

There are words buried inside her — oceans of words that never reach the shore.
When she tries to speak, society labels her "disrespectful."
When she tries to argue, they call her "arrogant."
   She is told not to go beyond boys.
She is told not to dream bigger than her husband.
She is told not to stand taller than her brother.
   But she is the voice of that mother who raised every man.
She is the woman of that house who has kept it safe through storms.
She is the body full of scars who still dresses her pain in silence.
   Even when her soul is wounded, she carries her dreams like a prayer tied in her heart.
She sees women like her dying inside every day —
and yet she still trusts every man.
   That's not weakness.
That's divinity disguised as endurance.

FOUR
THE BROKEN FAITH

She knows the irony of her life.
She nurtures the very man who will question her tomorrow.
She feeds the same world that starves her of respect.
She loves the same society that doesn't love her back.
   The point is not about rights.
It's about recognition — to be seen as a person.
But in this race to prove who's better,
man and woman have both stopped being human.
   Now, everyone is fighting to win a war that kills them both.
We've become a battlefield of egos —
male ego, female ego — no empathy left, only comparison.
   We don't listen anymore.
We compete in pain.
And in that competition, both are dying.
Men are losing peace.
Women are losing freedom.
And humanity is losing its soul.

FIVE
THE SOCIAL PRISON

This society has turned into a silent killer.
It doesn't murder with knives — it murders with judgment.
It doesn't hang people — it hangs their self-respect.
    On social media, people pretend to care,
but their eyes are dirty and their hearts are empty.
They comment on her photos, not on her pain.
They measure her morality by her clothes,
and her worth by her silence.
    Here no one is truly right or wrong.
Every woman is blamed for playing with a man's heart.
Every man is blamed for destroying a woman's life.
And in this endless circle of blame —
truth dies quietly in the middle.

SIX
THE WOUNDS YOU DON'T SEE

You cannot always see a woman's scars.
They are not always on her body —
they live in her silence, her hesitation, her forced smile.

    She is that woman who cried all night and still woke up to pack tiffins.
She is that woman who hides her depression behind makeup.
She is that woman who apologizes even when it's not her fault.

    Her back carries generations of unspoken pain.
Her hands have built empires of men who forgot her name.
And yet, she still loves. She still forgives. She still believes.

    She keeps faith in the same world that calls her impure for speaking truth.
She is called bold for showing confidence,
and shameless for showing strength.

    No one asks her,
    "What happened?"
They only say,
"Don't talk about it."

    Her voice was never weak.
It was stolen.

SEVEN
THE CAGED DREAMS

There are countless skies waiting for her flight.
But her feet are tied by invisible chains —
made of family honor, society's rules, and men's fragile pride.
  She wants to study, they stop her.
She wants to work, they shame her.
She wants to travel, they scare her.
She wants to speak, they silence her.
  And yet, every night before she sleeps,
she closes her eyes and dreams —
dreams of running, flying, breathing freely.
  She knows her dream may never come true,
but she dreams anyway — because hope is her rebellion.

EIGHT
THE GOD WHO FAILED

No one needs change in this society anymore.
We are comfortable in our cruelty.
We think God made us perfect,
but we've become the biggest mistake of creation.
    God gave us hearts to feel,
but we turned them into stones.
God gave us minds to think,
but we filled them with judgment.
    Behind His back,
we are doing the very things that make Him weep —
hurting, breaking, killing humanity itself.
    We call ourselves humans,
but our behavior has made even the devil ashamed.

NINE

THE WOMAN AS THE WORLD

I am not writing this for sympathy.
I am writing this because I am that woman —
the one who raised the man who now rules the world.
    I am the fire that burns quietly.
I am the storm you cannot cage.
I am the blood that built your dynasty.
    You can call me mother, sister, daughter, wife —
but first, call me what I am — human.
    I don't want your pity.
I want your awareness.
I don't want your pedestal.
I want equality.
    My existence is not decoration.
It's the foundation.
    Without me, there is no creation,
no compassion,
no continuity.
    So when you ask why a woman's existence is important,
look around —
every heartbeat, every breath, every soul began inside her.

TEN

HER VOICE WILL NOT DIE

Today, she may still walk through shadows.
But she walks.
Even when her feet bleed, she walks.
    Every woman who speaks her truth
adds one more crack to the walls of silence.
One day, those walls will fall —
and her voice will echo through every generation.
    Because you can silence a woman,
but you can't kill her truth.
You can ignore her cries,
but you can't stop her fire.
    She is not half.
She is the whole we never acknowledged.
    She is the silent half —
but not for long.

ELEVEN

THE UNSEEN HUMAN

People no longer see a woman as human.
They see her as a helper, a role, a label.
She can cook, she can clean, she can obey — but if she dreams, she's called shameless.
If she argues, she's called disrespectful.
　　Every man was raised by a woman.
Every heart that beats today, beats because of her.
Yet when she asks for respect, society says — "Why do you need more?"
　　She was never asking for more.
She was asking for what was already hers — dignity.

TWELVE
THE SILENCE OF HER VOICE

There are words in her heart that never reach her lips.
When she speaks, people laugh.
When she cries, people call her weak.
When she stays silent, they call her fake.
    Her voice is like a river — it flows, but it's always stopped by the dam of tradition.
Society has made her believe that obedience is virtue and silence is peace.
But obedience is not peace.
Silence is not respect.
    A woman's silence is a graveyard of unspoken dreams.
And in that graveyard, humanity has buried its conscience.

THIRTEEN
THE BODY THAT CARRIES THE WORLD

Her body is not a temple; it's a battlefield.
It carries scars of labor, of pain, of violence, of unwanted touch, of childbirth, of shame.
She carries wounds that no medicine can heal —
because the disease is not in her, it is in us.
People look at her body before they look at her eyes.
They praise her shape, not her strength.
They comment on her beauty, not her bravery.
And when she covers herself, they mock her.
When she doesn't, they judge her.
No matter what she does, she is wrong —
because the world is not built to accept her,
it is built to control her.

FOURTEEN
THE DOMESTIC PRISON

A woman's home is often her cage.
They tell her, "This is your world."
But her world has walls, not skies.
She cooks, cleans, cares, listens, sacrifices —
and at the end of the day, she is told, "You did nothing extraordinary."
   She wakes up before everyone, sleeps after everyone,
and yet, her worth is measured in how quietly she suffers.
   No one counts her exhaustion.
No one thanks her for her endurance.
Her love is expected, not appreciated.
Her labor is demanded, not respected.
   Every meal she cooks is made from pain.
Every smile she wears is stitched with restraint.
And every time she is told to be "a good woman,"
a part of her dies quietly.

FIFTEEN
THE SOCIETY OF DOUBLE FACES

Society worships goddesses but disrespects women.
They build temples for Durga, Kali, Lakshmi —
but insult the living women in their own homes.
   They say, "A woman should be pure."
But they never define what purity means.
Is purity silence?
Is purity suffering?
Is purity never saying "no"?
   They celebrate her when she sacrifices,
but condemn her when she stands for herself.
   This is the society that touches feet and breaks hearts in the same breath.
This is the culture that blesses daughters but cages them when they start dreaming.

SIXTEEN
THE MOTHER WHO RAISED THE WORLD

I am the voice of that mother who raised every man.
Her hands are wrinkled with work,
her heart heavy with patience.

She never studied philosophy,
but she taught the world what love means.

She gave birth in pain,
raised children in hunger,
and still smiled like the sun.

She is the only person who gives without expecting anything in return —
and yet she is blamed for not being enough.

She raised men who forgot how to respect women.
She raised daughters who learned to hide their emotions.
And still, she never blamed anyone —
because that's what mothers do.

SEVENTEEN
THE SHAME SHE NEVER ASKED FOR

Every woman walks with fear stitched to her shadow.
When she leaves home, she looks behind.
When she walks on the street, she lowers her gaze.
When she returns, she locks the door twice.
   The world has made her safety her responsibility.
When she is harassed, they ask,
   "What was she wearing?"
"Why was she outside at night?"
   They never ask the man,
   "Why did you look?"
"Why did you touch?"
   This is the hypocrisy that burns her every day.
She carries shame she never earned,
and blame she never deserved.

EIGHTEEN
THE EDUCATION SHE WAS DENIED

Knowledge is freedom.
But they told her — "Girls don't need too much education."
Because educated girls ask questions.
And questions disturb the comfort of the powerful.
   Her dreams were replaced with marriage proposals.
Her textbooks were replaced with recipes.
Her pen was taken away,
and her voice was called rebellion.
   She wasn't afraid of knowledge.
Society was.

NINETEEN
THE SOCIAL MEDIA CIRCUS

Now, the world hides behind screens.
People talk about women's rights with hashtags
and violate them with comments.
  They post "Respect Women" in stories,
and send insults in DMs.
They share quotes about empowerment,
but still stare at her body in pictures.
  This generation doesn't need new rules —
it needs new hearts.
Because no law can fix what the soul refuses to understand.

TWENTY
THE WOMAN AS THE WARRIOR

Despite everything, she rises.
Despite every scar, she shines.
Despite every betrayal, she believes.
   She carries the world in her womb,
and the universe in her strength.
   She is not delicate.
She is divine.
   She may cry,
but her tears are weapons.
She may fall,
but every fall turns into her next rise.
   She has learned that freedom is not given — it is claimed.
And she is claiming it, step by step, voice by voice, heart by heart

TWENTY-ONE
THE WOMAN AND THE GOD

If there is God,
He exists in her forgiveness.
In her love that never ends.
In her sacrifice that never asks.
  God gave man life,
but it was woman who kept it alive.
  She doesn't want to be worshipped.
She wants to be respected.
She doesn't want to be above anyone.
She wants to stand beside everyone.

TWENTY-TWO
THE REBIRTH OF HER VOICE

Her time is coming.
The silence is cracking.
The whispers are turning into roars.
  One woman speaks — and a thousand more rise.
One girl dreams — and a thousand more dare.
Her voice is no longer hidden.
It is echoing through generations.
  She is not asking to be heard —
she is demanding to be understood.

TWENTY-THREE
THE WOMAN IS THE WORLD

Without her, the world collapses.
Without her, love doesn't exist.
Without her, even God is incomplete.
   She is not the weaker sex.
She is the entire existence disguised in tenderness.
   Every wound she carries is a lesson.
Every tear she sheds is a prayer.
Every dream she chases is the future itself.
   She is woman —
not half of the world,
but the whole that keeps it alive.

TWENTY-FOUR
SUFFER LONG

This is not fiction.
These words come from the wounds of countless women who breathe, bleed, and still smile in a world that measures their worth by how quietly they suffer.
It is not a tale to be read; it is a mirror to be felt.
Because every scar a woman hides is a story society never wanted to hear.

TWENTY-FIVE
THE BENEATH

People nowadays do not consider a woman as a human being.
They call her strong only when she swallows her pain. They call her weak when she dares to cry.
She becomes everything — a wife, a mother, a sister, a worker — yet, somehow, never herself.
   They told her:
"You can do household work."
"You can take care of children."
"You can listen to every argument in the world."
   But who decided that she must?
Did a single man create this rule, or did all of us let it happen silently?

TWENTY-SIX
THE VOICE BENEATH THE SILENCE

She stands before the mirror — her face calm, her hands trembling. The reflection shows a woman dressed neatly, but her eyes carry the stories of sleepless nights and unspoken screams.

The world calls her strong.
But strength, here, is another word for endurance — endurance of pain, of humiliation, of endless expectations.

She whispers to herself:
"I am the voice of that mother who raised every man."
And in that moment, she is every woman.

TWENTY-SEVEN
THE CHAINS OF EXPECTATION

From the moment she was born, her life was written —
"You are a girl, and you should work like a girl."

Her toys were utensils, her dreams stitched inside saree folds, her laughter caged behind "be careful."

No one asked her what she wanted to become.
They only taught her what she should not become.

She cooked dreams while making rotis.
She learned silence while others spoke of freedom.
And when she cried, they said, "That's what women do."

But no one asked why.

TWENTY-EIGHT
THE SCARS THEY NEVER SEE

*She has scars — not the ones that bleed, but the ones that burn in silence.
Scars that come from words, not whips.
From glances, not blows.*

Every night, she hides her pain under the same dupatta that is meant to "protect her."

She remembers the times she was told:
"Don't laugh too loud, people will think you are shameless."
"Don't argue, you are a woman."
"Don't dream too big, you'll forget your duties."

Her body is whole, but her soul... has been bruised a thousand times.

TWENTY-NINE
THE UNHEARD CRIES

When a woman screams in pain, the world lowers its volume.
When a woman speaks in truth, the world calls her disrespectful.
   She carries the cries of many — the wife silenced by her husband's temper,
the daughter told she's a burden,
the working woman blamed for being too ambitious,
and the victim told, "It must have been your fault."
   Their voices merge into one —
a storm trapped inside the hollow chest of society

THIRTY
THE BODY THAT CARRIES SHAME

Every woman's body is treated like a battlefield.
They dress her, undress her, judge her, shame her.
If she covers, they call her old-fashioned.
If she doesn't, they call her characterless.
  And yet, they forget —
this body has birthed kings,
has carried pain without complaint,
has nurtured even those who destroy it.
  Still, she walks —
through streets that bite her dignity,
through eyes that undress her every second,
and she still finds courage to smile.

THIRTY-ONE
THE DREAMS IN CHAINS

Her dreams are not loud; they are whispers drowned in kitchen sounds.
She once wanted to paint,
but they handed her a broom.
She once wanted to fly,
but they tied her wings with "log kya kahenge."
Still, she dreams.
Because dreams are her rebellion.
Every time she prays, she doesn't ask for luxury —
she asks for freedom.
Freedom to walk, to breathe, to exist without fear.

THIRTY-TWO
THE BROKEN SOCIETY

Society — that invisible monster — feeds on hypocrisy.
It preaches purity to women, but protects men who destroy it.
It builds walls for daughters and doors for sons.
   Here, social media is the new god —
where people worship filters but hide their cruelty.
Where a woman's worth is measured by likes,
and her dignity destroyed by comments.
   No one here is pure —
every man who mocks a woman,
every woman who stays silent —
all are part of this rot.

THIRTY-THREE
THE WOMAN WHO STILL BELIEVES

And yet...
she believes.
In love.
In men.
In goodness.
   Even after being broken by those she trusted,
she still feeds the same world that bruised her.
   Because she is the mother,
the nurturer,
the quiet builder of civilizations.
   She knows that every man, no matter how cruel,
was once held by a woman's hand.
And yet, she forgives.
   That is her strength — not her weakness.

THIRTY-FOUR
THE FIRE INSIDE

The time for silence has ended.
Now her voice is not a whisper — it's thunder.
   She no longer wants pity,
she wants respect.
   She doesn't want to rise above men,
she wants to rise beside them.
   Because equality is not about who's stronger —
it's about who's human.
   She stands on the ruins of old rules,
and her eyes burn with the fire of every woman who was told to "stay quiet."
   Now, she speaks.
And the world trembles.

THIRTY-FIVE
THE MIRROR OF HUMANITY

The question remains —
who created this society?
   A man?
A woman?
Or both, lost in their egos?
   We are fighting among ourselves,
while forgetting that both man and woman were made by the same God.
   In trying to prove who is better,
we forgot to be human.
And that, perhaps, is the greatest tragedy of all.

THIRTY-SIX
THE WOMAN WHO RISES

She rises.
Not as a victim,
but as a creator of her destiny.
   Her scars are her medals.
Her pain is her poetry.
Her silence is her storm.
   She is not asking for a place — she is creating one.
   And the world, for once, must listen.

THIRTY-SEVEN
THE WOMAN AND THE SKY

There are still empty skies to fly.
But her feet are chained by rules written in dust.
    She looks up,
smiles softly,
and whispers —
    "You can chain my feet, but not my dreams."
    Because she is every woman —
the mother, the warrior, the dreamer,
the broken one who still heals others.
    Her existence is not a question —
it is the answer to why humanity still exists.

THIRTY-EIGHT
THE UNHEARD HEARTBEAT

In a dark room lit by a dim bulb, she sits quietly.
Her hands move — washing, cleaning, folding, caring.
But her mind screams stories that no one will ever hear.

The world sees her — but never looks at her.
They say she has everything: a family, a home, respect.
Yet, deep inside, she knows — she is living as a shadow of herself.

Her reflection whispers, "You were born free, but they taught you to serve."
And that's where her story begins.

THIRTY-NINE
THE BIRTH OF EXPECTATION

The moment she was born, someone whispered,
"It's a girl."
The tone was not joy — it was a sigh.
Before she could breathe, she was already measured.
Before she could walk, her path was decided.
They said, "She will grow up to take care of her husband."
They said, "She will make her family proud — by sacrifice."
No one said, "She will make herself proud."
That's where the first scar formed — invisible, silent, eternal.

FORTY
THE WEIGHT OF DUTY

Every morning begins with service —
To the home, to the husband, to the world.
  She becomes the sun, but no one notices her light.
Her hands, cracked from endless work,
still hold warmth for everyone except herself.
  Her dreams sit quietly beside the stove,
burning little by little,
turning to smoke that no one sees.

FORTY-ONE
THE INVISIBLE SCARS

They say wounds heal with time.
But some wounds never bleed — they just exist.
Her scars are not on her skin.
They are in the words thrown like stones —
"Don't speak too much."
"Don't dream too big."
"Don't look up when you walk."
Each "don't" became a wall.
And she built her life inside those walls,
decorated it with silence,
called it home.

FORTY-TWO
THE STOLEN DREAMS

Once, she wanted to dance.
Once, she wanted to write.
Once, she wanted to fly.
  But dreams are luxury for men —
for women, dreams are rebellion.
  Every time she reached out,
someone pulled her back with the rope of "tradition."
  And so, she learned to dream only in her sleep —
where no one could stop her.

FORTY-THREE
THE BODY AND THE BURDEN

Her body is not hers — it belongs to judgment.
It belongs to eyes that weigh, mouths that whisper, and rules that choke.
   If she covers herself, they call her conservative.
If she doesn't, they call her shameless.
If she speaks, she's loud.
If she's quiet, she's weak.
   She learns that womanhood is not beauty — it's battle.
A war fought daily, between her dignity and their opinions.

FORTY-FOUR
THE CHAOS OF SOCIETY

Who made this society?
No one knows.
But everyone follows it like a god.
    Here, men preach respect and practice hypocrisy.
Here, women are taught to judge each other to survive.
Here, social media decides who's pure and who's polluted.
    It is not a society anymore — it's a circus of morality.
And in the middle of it stands a woman,
bleeding silently while the crowd claps.

FORTY-FIVE
THE WOMAN WHO STILL LOVES

Despite the pain, she still gives love.
Despite betrayal, she still forgives.
Despite cruelty, she still smiles.
   Because she is made of something divine —
not softness, but sacrifice.
   She loves even those who destroy her,
because she knows that hate only multiplies the wound.
Love, for her, is not emotion — it's survival.

FORTY-SIX
THE BROKEN VOICES

Every woman has a story —
the girl who was told to stay home,
the mother who lost herself raising others,
the widow who still fights loneliness in silence.
   Their voices are ghosts that live inside walls,
in whispers of prayers and silent sobs.
   When one woman cries,
a hundred others feel the same pain in their bones.
   Because womanhood is not just a body —
it's a shared ache that runs through generations.

FORTY-SEVEN
THE RAGE OF RESURRECTION

But one day, silence bursts.
One day, the quiet woman says no.
   Her eyes stop fearing,
her hands stop trembling,
her words start cutting through stone.
   She is no longer a victim —
she becomes a storm.
   And that storm does not destroy — it cleanses.
It washes away centuries of submission
and gives birth to the new woman —
fierce, fearless, and free.

FORTY-EIGHT
THE FIRE OF CHANGE

*Change does not come from speeches.
It comes from tears that decide to turn into rebellion.
   Every woman who stands up,
every girl who says "I will not stop,"
is a revolution wrapped in flesh.
   And slowly, one by one,
they start lighting candles in this dark society.
Every flame is a woman,
and together they burn the darkness.*

FORTY-NINE
THE MEN WHO LEARNED

Not all men are monsters.
Some are broken mirrors too,
shaped by the same society that taught them power is dominance.
  And when these men finally listen — truly listen —
they begin to heal alongside women.
  Because the future is not man versus woman —
it is man with woman.
Together, they can create what history failed to:
a world where empathy is not weakness,
and equality is not a threat.

FIFTY

THE WOMAN AND THE SKY

Now she looks up again.
The sky no longer looks distant — it looks possible.
   Her feet still carry the chains,
but her soul has learned to fly through them.
   She whispers,
"You can wound my body, but never my will."
   Her scars shine — not as marks of pain,
but as symbols of victory.
   Because she didn't just survive —
she transformed.

FIFTY-ONE
BORN TO SHINE

She was not born to serve,
She was born to shine —
But the world dimmed her light
And called it destiny.

FIFTY-TWO
HER SILENCE

They say her silence is peace,
But silence screams louder
When the world refuses to hear her name.

FIFTY-THREE
HIDES A STORM

Behind every smile she wears,
There hides a storm —
Not of tears,
But of strength no one noticed.

FIFTY-FOUR
CARRY STORIES

Her eyes carry stories
Of love that never returned,
Of dreams that died quietly
So others could live loudly.

FIFTY-FIVE
WRAPPED IN SKIN

She is fire wrapped in skin,
Soft to touch,
But fierce when broken.

FIFTY-SIX
SHE REWROTE

Every scar on her body
Is a sentence the world wrote,
But every heartbeat she owns
Is a word she rewrote.

FIFTY-SEVEN
SILENCE GROW

They tried to bury her voice,
But forgot —
She was a seed,
And silence only made her grow.

FIFTY-EIGHT
STRENGTH IS A LIE

She cooks, she cleans, she cries, she dreams —
And still, they call her weak.
If weakness built the world,
Then strength is a lie.

FIFTY-NINE
CHAINED HER FEET

They chained her feet,
But her thoughts still wandered
Beyond the sky —
Because dreams don't wear anklets.

SIXTY
UNSPOKEN PRAYERS

Her tears are not water,
They are history —
Every drop carrying
A thousand unspoken prayers.

SIXTY-ONE
REBIRTH

She has died a hundred times
In the same body,
And still she wakes
As if rebirth is her habit.

SIXTY-TWO
I AM THE HOME

They told her —
"You belong to home."
She answered —
"I am the home."

SIXTY-THREE
POURS KINDNESS

Even after betrayal,
She pours kindness.
Even after pain,
She gives peace.
She is not fragile —
She is faith, reborn.

SIXTY-FOUR
AGAINST SILENCE

When she raises her voice,
It is not against men —
It is against silence.

SIXTY-FIVE
READ BY THE BLIND

Every woman is a poem
Written by struggle,
Edited by sacrifice,
And read by the blind.

SIXTY-SIX
BECOMES THE ARROW

The world breaks her
To see how much she can bend.
But she bends like a bow —
And every time she rises,
She becomes the arrow.

SIXTY-SEVEN
EQUAL TO THE SKY

—•♡•—

She was never asking to rule —
Only to be seen
As equal to the sky she breathes.

SIXTY-EIGHT
HER EMOTIONAL

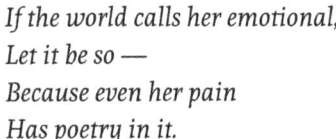

If the world calls her emotional,
Let it be so —
Because even her pain
Has poetry in it.

SIXTY-NINE
HEARTBEAT OF HUMANITY

She doesn't need saving.
She needs to be heard.
Because inside her chest
Lives the heartbeat of humanity.

SEVENTY
SOUND OF SURVIVAL

She is not a story of sorrow —
She is the sound of survival.

SEVENTY-ONE
MEANING OF FREEDOM

The day she stopped apologizing,
The world learned the meaning of freedom.

SEVENTY-TWO
HER PAST

They burned her past,
But forgot —
Ashes also tell stories
If you have the heart to listen.

SEVENTY-THREE
HEAVEN BOWS

When she cries,
The earth listens.
When she rises,
Heaven bows.

SEVENTY-FOUR
BEGINING OF LOVE

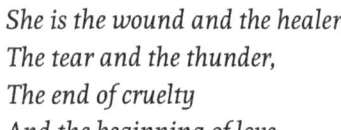

She is the wound and the healer,
The tear and the thunder,
The end of cruelty
And the beginning of love.

Epilogue – The Eternal Woman

There are many names for her —
mother, sister, wife, daughter.
But before all that,
she is human.
The day we stop dividing her into roles,
and start seeing her as a person,
is the day humanity will rise again.
Her voice is no longer a cry —
it's a song,
a hymn of existence that echoes across time:
"I am not a burden. I am not a weakness.
I am the reason you exist.
I am the woman — the beginning, the bridge, and the sky."

Made in the USA
Monee, IL
03 May 2026

49437772R00059